Cindy Football Boots

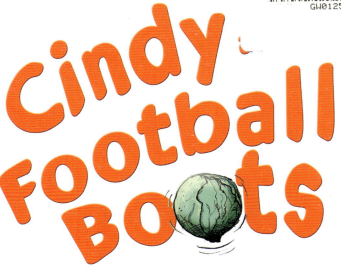

Written by Jan Burchett & Sara Vogler

Illustrated by Sholto Walker

Chapter 1

Cindy loved playing football. But Duncan and Dean, her stepbrothers, wouldn't let her play with them. She was a lot better than they were! So Cindy used to practise by herself at home.

"I don't know how she does that!" Duncan complained to Dean as they watched her dribbling a cabbage expertly round the garden. "She hasn't even got boots on."

"She hasn't got any boots, doughnut head!" scoffed Dean.

Of course, Cindy desperately wanted some football boots but she didn't have enough pocket money. It was no good asking Dad, either. He never had any spare cash, even though he worked such long hours.

One morning Cindy was heading a bag of pasta up the hall, when a leaflet fluttered through the letterbox. Dean leapt out of the lounge and grabbed it.

"FOOTBALL TRIALS FOR NEW YOUTH TEAM!" he read.

Duncan sprinted down the stairs and snatched the paper from him.

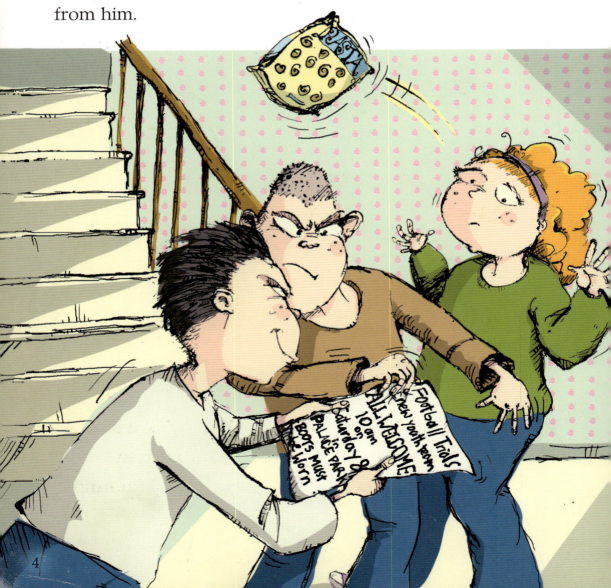

"I'm the best defender there is," boasted Dean. "They'll be begging me to play!"

"Don't be a baboon brain!" sneered Duncan. "They'll be so dazzled by my tackling they won't even know you're there."

Dean bashed Duncan with the bag of pasta. Duncan whacked Dean with a cushion. Soon there was a blizzard of pasta and feathers.

Cindy picked up the leaflet. Wow! This was the chance she had been waiting for. She imagined herself dribbling down the field ... dodging defenders ... slamming the ball into the back of the net ... winning the cup!

Cindy would go to the trials and nothing would stop her.

"I can't wait till Saturday!"

Duncan and Dean gawped at her open-mouthed.

"You can't go!" they spluttered.

"Why not?" asked Cindy.

Duncan and Dean got into a huddle.

"If she goes to the trials we won't stand a chance!" whispered Duncan.

"Think of a way to stop her then," hissed Dean.

They turned to Cindy.

"You can't go because you're a girl," Duncan told her.

"It says all welcome," said Cindy.

"Well you're not tall enough," said Dean desperately.

"It doesn't say you have to be measured," laughed Cindy.

Duncan snatched the leaflet and peered at it closely. Then his eyes lit up. "You can't go," he sneered. "It says here football boots must be worn."

"And you haven't got any!" sniggered Dean.

When Cindy woke up on Saturday morning she felt extremely miserable. Dad had gone to work and Duncan and Dean were strutting about getting ready for the trials.

"Where're my shin pads?" demanded Dean.

"Who's got my lucky shirt?" yelled Duncan from upstairs.

"Clean my boots, Cindy," ordered Dean, plonking them on the kitchen table.

Cindy started scrubbing mud off the boots.

"Maybe I'll just come and watch then," she mumbled.

Dean turned as white as his shirt.

"If we see you anywhere near those trials, you'll be sorry," he growled, snatching up his boots. "Come on, Duncan. Let's go!"

The boys sprinted out of the house, slamming the door behind them.

Cindy plonked herself down at the kitchen table and sank her head into her hands. It wasn't fair. She was too good at football to spend her time kicking vegetables round the garden. She should be at the trials.

Then she heard a tapping at the kitchen window. It was Fay who lived next door. Cindy hurriedly wiped her eyes and let her in.

"Hello dear, can I borrow some…" Fay stopped and looked at Cindy's crumpled face.

"What's wrong?" she asked kindly.

Cindy told her the whole story. "If only I had some football boots," she finished with a sob, "I could take part in the trials."

"Football boots," said Fay thoughtfully. "I might be able to help you there! Back in a tick." With that she vanished.

And before you could say Michael Owen she was back – holding a pair of football boots!

"These belonged to my boy Bobby," she told Cindy. "If they fit, you can keep them."

Cindy pulled on the clumpy old boots. They went right over her ankles and had thick black laces. But they fitted perfectly!

"Thank you!" breathed Cindy.

"Well don't just stand there," laughed Fay. "You've got some trials to attend. Just make sure you're home before those stepbrothers of yours."

Chapter 2

Cindy stood half-hidden at the park gate, the old brown boots concealed in a plastic bag. She spotted her stepbrothers amongst an eager crowd of children. Whatever happened, Duncan and Dean mustn't see her.

   Cindy thrust her hair up under her woolly hat and smeared some mud on her face. Then she pulled her boots on and ran onto the pitch.

Duncan and Dean sniggered when they saw the strange player in the ancient brown boots.

"Where d'you think he got those boots?" scoffed Dean.

"From a dustbin!" sneered Duncan.

A whistle blew. The man in charge called everyone over.

"I'm Steve Prince," he grinned, waving a clipboard. "Once you've all signed up we can start the trials. Then I'll pick my squad and the Palace Park Panthers will be ready for action!"

Cindy couldn't risk adding her name to the list.

Mr Prince watched the play very closely. There were so many children for him to see that Cindy wondered if he'd ever get round to her.

At last she was on the pitch. She didn't have long to prove herself – and be home before her stepbrothers.

Cindy took up her position in midfield. To her dismay Duncan and Dean were playing for the opposing team.

Cindy soon got possession of the ball. With a clever toe punt she passed it across the field and shot off like a rocket up the wing. The boots felt amazing!

Now the ball was sailing towards her again. She controlled it and made for the goal.

Out of the corner of her eye she could see Duncan skidding towards her, both feet aimed at her shins instead of the ball. He was going to bring her down!

Cindy was ready for him. She tapped the ball cleverly to the side, skipped over Duncan's legs and carried on with her run. She could hear Duncan yelling.

"That's cheating! Send him off!"

Now the goal was in sight. But someone was lumbering over to block her way. It was Dean!

Dean charged at her with his arms out, ready to knock her to the ground. Cindy chipped the ball over his head and darted round him. Dean was so surprised he fell over. "You pushed me!" he whined.

Cindy pressed forward. The goalie came out to meet her. She dodged to the left and, as the goalkeeper dived, she curled the ball skilfully into the back of the net.

Mr Prince blew his whistle. "That was brilliant!" he called. "What's your name?"

Cindy was delighted! As she approached Mr Prince, she glanced around and realised the trials were over. She had to get home! Snatching up her trainers she turned to run, but one of her boots got stuck in the mud. In a panic she wrenched her foot out of it and ran on, leaving the boot behind.

"Come back!" called Mr Prince. But she had vanished. Then he noticed Cindy's boot in the mud. He picked it up.

Cindy made it home just before her stepbrothers. Duncan and Dean were in a foul mood. As soon as Dad put his key in the door, they started complaining about the trials and how unfair it had all been. Cindy kept herself busy peeling potatoes so no one would see her crying. She'd lost one of her precious boots and Mr Prince didn't even know who she was. She'd never be in the team now.

Twenty minutes later there was a knock at the front door. It was Mr Prince! Dad showed him into the lounge.

"It's about the football trials," he explained. "I'm visiting all the kids on my list. I want the player who left this boot behind to be in my team. Does it belong to Duncan or Dean?"

When Cindy saw her missing boot she almost dropped the potato. Before she could speak, Duncan grabbed the boot and tried to ram his foot in it.

"It's mine!" he said. "I'm the one you want."

"Doughnut head!" scoffed Dean. "You can't get half your foot in. It's my boot." He snatched it from Duncan.

Duncan thumped him. "Baboon brain! You can't even get your big toe in."

"I don't understand. These are the last names on my list," sighed Mr Prince.

Cindy stepped forward. "It's my boot," she said shyly.

"But you weren't even there!" shouted Duncan.

"We wouldn't let her go," smirked Dean.

"I'll deal with you two later," said Dad firmly. "Is it your boot, Cindy?"

"Yes," said Cindy. "And I've got the other one here to prove it." Cindy pulled on the boots and did keep-it-up all round the lounge with the potato.

"I didn't know you were good at football!" gasped Dad.

"She's not just good," said Mr Prince. "She's brilliant. In fact she's going to be my star player."